# YORKSHIRE

*by*

## LEN MARKHAM

COUNTRYSIDE BOOKS

NEWBURY · BERKSHIRE

COUNTRYSIDE BOOKS
3 Catherine Road
Newbury, Berkshire

ISBN  1  85306  443  2

Produced through MRM Associates Ltd., Reading
Printed by Woolnough Bookbinding Ltd., Irthlingborough

# CONTENTS

'Beware of emptyng pysse pottes,
and pyssing in chymnes'

# FOREWORD

From our Neanderthal ancestors onwards, every human being that ever lived has, of necessity, performed the same bodily chore; the daily task of voiding waste products permitting no distinction between the king and the common man. Before the battle of Agincourt in 1415, the dysentery suffering Henry V and his army (which included a knot of Yorkshire bowmen) crouched in military order, each straining royal or ragamuffined cheek having little idea of the seating revolution yet to come.

The transition from al fresco evacuation to high-tech flush has been an evolutionary process, offering in the porcelained pristinity of today the ultimate in sanitised comfort. But somewhere along the way came the still acclaimed privy — a halfway house long remembered for its residential spiders and the supplementary education to be gleaned from tearings of the Sporting Pink. In the age of the waterless closet, alacrity with undergarments came as standard and yet the old privies evoke a certain nostalgia, being as synonymous with the 18th and early 19th century as Beechams Pills and bloomers.

So what happened to these chapels of ease? I made a few tentative enquiries and the gush of responses hit me like an unblocked drain! It would seem that many older Yorkshire folk regret the passing of their nettie, and thousands of even my own generation — we who grew up with donkey stones, shiny Izal toilet paper and rear ends congenitally accustomed to draughts and ice clad bowls — lament the disappearance of the outside loo. I certainly had no shortage of leads for this book. So off I went with a divining rod and a camera.

The result is this humble volume. A fireside read? Or would you rather browse in the bathroom?

Len Markham
Barwick-in-Elmet

'It went down there?' Little helpers inspecting a child's rocking chair commode outside the White House Folk Museum on Otley Chevin.

# [ 1 ]

## The Privy In History

Nomadic man had no need for organised methods of waste disposal. Like ruminant herds of wildebeest, he did it spontaneously on the hoof and it was not until the creation of permanent settlements that the need for more formalised arrangements became apparent.

Communal discharges assailed nose and eye, and, such were the quantities of excreta in the narrow spaces between buildings, that the wearing of sandals became a hazardous occupation, provoking the citizens of the ancient world into action. The Roman legions invaded Britain in AD 43 and along with their weapons of war they brought strange sponge-tipped sticks. For a while these perplexed the vanquished until all became clear when the legionaries were observed at their toilet, dedicating their offerings to Stercutius and Crepitus, the gods of ordure and convenience, and Cloacina, the goddess of the common sewer. In York and elsewhere in the county the Romans built public latrines with marble seats, often arranged in semi-circles over streams or specially constructed conduits. Here they sat taking their ease, discussing the affairs of empire with comrades, finally dipping their sticks into channels of water in front of the latrines or into phials of salt water as a prelude to cleansing.

When the Romans left, the personal hygiene of dozens of subsequent generations regressed. The Anglo-Saxons dug once-only latrine pits and the Vikings made do with similar holes in the ground surrounded by wattle fencing. The post-Norman period saw the introduction of more permanent dropping places – pits lined with limestone blocks or bricks to facilitate emptying, although the practice of tipping waste into the streets continued.

Falls of the Roman Empire – communal toilets in the Roman town of Salamis, Northern Cyprus. (Courtesy of H. Mayfield)

Re-civilising influences came from two sources – monastic and aristocratic.

In siting their grand religious houses, like Roche, Kirkstall,

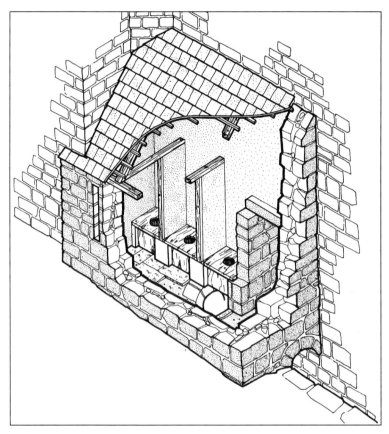

12th-century sophistication at Kirkstall Abbey near Leeds. An impression of the garderobes attached to the Chamber Block and set over the main drain. Note the removable wooden seats and front boards with which each cubicle was once furnished. Large numbers of metal lace-ends used as clothing fasteners have been found in the vicinity. (Drawing courtesy of West Yorkshire Archaeology Service)

Fountains and Jervaulx abbeys, the monks invariably chose sites close to rivers, building their reredorters over the flow. Subsequent castle architecture also took into account lavatorial needs. Projecting stone-seated privies were built high into the castle walls or in specifically designated garderobe towers. Occasionally, privies were accommodated within chimney breasts to afford some comfort to bare flesh and to enable foul odours to be expelled on the updraught. Gravity ensured that the nobility remained unsullied – and some projectiles were, it was reported, more effective than boiling oil in repelling attackers – but the droppings steadily accumulated and had to be removed. The task fell to the poetically named gong fermors. Employed regularly in large castles such as those at Richmond and Pontefract, these night workers toiled waist deep with buckets and scoops in appalling conditions, and although they were well paid (up to forty shillings for each job) their working lives could be short. In 1326, one distinguished scooper, by the name of Richard the Raker, fell through the rotten planks of a privy and drowned 'monstrously in his own excrement'.

In 1388 the first sanitary bill in British history was enacted, instructing that 'the townsfolk themselves should remove from the streets, all the dirt and filth.' Following this, communal privies were gradually introduced to the large towns. London was equipped with three such straining stations, the most famous being on London Bridge. It is estimated that old Father Thames spluttered in an annual morass of some 2,000 tons of human waste. So bad was the pollution that cloth sheets perfumed with lavender and roses had to be hung in the Houses of Parliament to 'stay' the smell. The malpractice of committing plops to the deep was widespread in Yorkshire for another 500 years, although enlightened legislators in Hull in 1576 ordered that the use of three privies projecting over the jetty at Horsestaithe had to be discontinued, 'for that the same privies are

10

High society — the 15th-century residents of the Marmion Gatehouse in West Tanfield used this projecting garderobe. Note the adjacent rainwater spout.

Garderobe shaft set into the 13th-century Cliffords Tower in York.

very noisome to the passengers in the ferry boat.' Until 1886 Sheffield sewage was discharged without treatment straight into the borough's rivers. The consequences for our conurbations were dire. Cholera, diarrhoea and other rampant diseases flourished in the unsanitary conditions and thousands of people died.

In the countryside, peasants were required to relieve themselves in the fields, 'a bow-shot away' from their humble dwellings. The privileged few, on the other hand, used velvet lipped buckets discreetly housed in boxes, the contents emptied daily by servants. Spending a groat continued in such rudimentary mode for hundreds of years. But why, given the salutary lessons of the Romans, did it take such a long time for the penny to drop? Drop it eventually did, and in 1596 the first true flushing water closet was invented by Sir John Harington for Queen Elizabeth.

However, the majestic personage was not amused. For a time she banned Harington from court, although he was reinstated and went on to install his contraption in Richmond Palace. But the idea was pooh-poohed, intermittent water supplies denying ordinary folk their conveniences for generations. Flushless, the next epoch has been christened in sanitary circles 'the Midden Ages'.

The common lot of the plebeian classes even up to the start of the present century was the fly-blown cesspit, ashpit or muckheap. Save for a roof to deflect raindrops and a perforated plank for backsides, the basic arrangements for defecating had scarcely changed since the era of the Norsemen and the Ouse settlement at Jorvik, although for the well-to-do there were concessions. One splendid privy built in 1702 at Castley Hall in Lower Wharfedale had a plastered, barrel-vaulted ceiling and two ranges of seats – probably four-holers. Another such distinguished structure, erected in Westerdale in 1711, has the following inscription chiselled over the portal:

13

The medieval loo in Monk Bar, York – some modern visitors cannot resist the temptation to drop their drawers!

14

## WHATSOEVER · THOU

## TAKEETH·IN·HAND

## REMEMBER·THY·END

Technology moved on and by 1775 an inventor by the name of Alexander Cummings had patented a closet bowl that held water fed from a cistern, the flow being controlled by a sliding valve. Three years later the immortal Joseph Bramah, whose surname is still a synonym for the nonpareil, gave us a much improved closet. Although such expensive devices were beyond the reach of the poor, improvements continued apace and, in 1845, the little known Edward Chrimes of Rotherham patented three new valve systems which brought significant savings in water consumption. Chrimes' pioneering inventions were followed in 1848 by legislative action. The Government, spurred by the work of Edwin Chadwick and his report *The General Report on the Sanitary Conditions of the Labouring Classes in Great Britain*, recognised the need to improve public health in the slums and it became mandatory for builders to provide fixed facilities in new houses – ash closets, privies or water closets. Also in this monumental year, a young Yorkshire lad of eleven left his Thorne home, bound on foot for London. The efforts of the eulogised Bramah left us a British superlative, but the lifetime work of Thomas Crapper has bequeathed an international term for the act itself.

The incomparable Thomas Crapper, and, being a fellow Yorkshireman, I will sing his praises, is known in some circles as the 'Barnes Wallace of the lavatory world'. Not so much an inventor, he was more a systems refiner and WC entrepreneur who developed a thriving business in London and became plumber to the King.

15

Earning four bob a week, Crapper began working for a master plumber in Chelsea. He was a hard working, dedicated and thrifty lad and, having thoroughly learned the trade, at the age of 24 he launched his own business. His Marlborough Works in Chelsea were inundated with orders, the demand for WCs prompted by the expanding network of metropolitan sewers. Crapper improved cistern design and, responding to the outcry over the profligate wastage of water associated with inefficient outlet valves, he delivered to the world his masterpiece:

Crapper's Valveless Waste Preventer.
One Moveable Part Only. Certain Flush With Easy Pull.
Will Flush When Only Two-Thirds Full.

In the best traditions of Empire, without fear of life or limb, the prototypes were fully tested in the factory, the swilling power of the new device coping with a variety of slop substitutes – apples, sponges, cotton waste, grease, 'air vessels' (these no doubt simulated certain rubber goods whose necks were often knotted by gentlemen) and an apprentice's cap, snatched from an unexpecting head and tossed into the contraption with the triumphant cry 'It works!' Crapper was exultant and convinced that his machine could conquer all, although there were doubting Thomases. The acid test came at the Hygiene Exhibition of 1884 in London. 'Surely the machine will choke on this lot?'

10 apples averaging $1\frac{3}{4}$ inch diameter
1 flat sponge $4\frac{1}{2}$ inch diameter
3 'air vessels'
plumber's smudge coated over the pan
4 pieces of paper adhering closely to the soiled surface

It didn't.

16

Crapper opened his opulent showrooms in King's Road, Chelsea.

Crapper's fame spread and he soon received a royal decree to install drains and bathrooms in Sandringham. Attention to detail was of the highest order, the specifications for the business ends including toilet seats in cedar, a sympathetic timber that was warmer to the skin than conventional mahogany. Soon every Tom, Dick and King Harry wanted one of Crapper's wizard machines and he eventually went on to be awarded four royal warrants by Edward VII and George V. He was immensely proud of the patronage, displaying the ultimate accolade of his achievements in a 6ft × 4ft royal crest above his Chelsea works.

Ever the entrepreneur, Crapper later joined forces with a lavatory pan specialist, Thomas Twyford of Stoke-on-Trent. Together the pair produced a Unitas pedestal closet, one of the first units going into Doncaster's Angel Hotel, where it had a champagne launch. Whilst on a visit to the town, Queen Victoria called in at the pub for a quick one and there was an instant clamour for a commemorative plaque. Even with the utmost textual decorum, however, the proposed sign hardly had the éclat of 'Queen Victoria Slept Here' and the plans were abandoned. Anxious to capitalise on Her Majesty's visit, the landlord was disappointed. But he need not have worried – as soon as the word got out, queues of Doncaster ladies were suddenly taken short.

In the 1880s Crapper grappled with the problems of sewer gases. Offensive to the nose and lethal if inhaled or ignited, these gases were the subject of intense experimentation, the back migration of odours finally being thwarted by the introduction of the U bend. How we take such ingenuity for granted! Our compatriot also developed the Trough Closet. Designed for institutions, workhouses and factories, these closets consisted of rows of toilets flushing into a common channel underneath. The calculations and principles were worked out with Crapper's

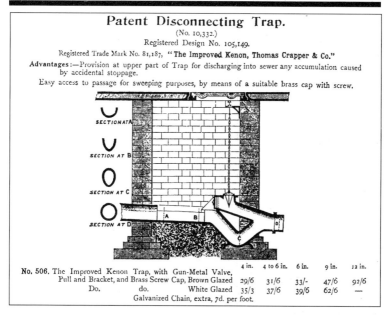

**Patent Disconnecting Trap.**

(No. 10,332.)

Registered Design No. 105,149.

Registered Trade Mark No. 81,187, "**The Improved Kenon, Thomas Crapper & Co.**"

**Advantages :**—Provision at upper part of Trap for discharging into sewer any accumulation caused by accidental stoppage.

Easy access to passage for sweeping purposes, by means of a suitable brass cap with screw.

SECTION AT A
SECTION AT B
SECTION AT C
SECTION AT D

| | | 4 in. | 4 to 6 in. | 6 in. | 9 in. | 12 in. |
|---|---|---|---|---|---|---|
| **No. 506.** The Improved Kenon Trap, with Gun-Metal Valve, Pull and Bracket, and Brass Screw Cap, Brown Glazed | | 29/6 | 31/6 | 33/- | 47/6 | 92/6 |
| Do. | do. White Glazed | 35/3 | 37/6 | 39/6 | 62/6 | — |
| Galvanized Chain, extra, 7d. per foot. | | | | | | |

Crapper was an innovator above and below ground.

usual thoroughness, but the master had not reckoned with the devilment of certain workhouse boys who, taking the opportunity of emulating Drake's incendiary heroics in defeating the Armada, sailed flaming paper boats upstream, leaving their neighbours screaming in agony.

After a lifetime of achievement, Crapper died in 1910 at the age of 73. Nearly a century on, I wonder about his less than respectful place in history. Who knows, if his mechanical bent had embraced say motor bike design, the term 'going for a crap' might have taken on a far more romantic meaning.

The new fangled contraptions of Crapper and his contemporaries were fine for the rich folk, but what about the workers! Inventions are all very well if you have the wherewithal to pay for them and in the late 19th and early 20th century in Yorkshire

'The incomparable Thomas Crapper.' (Victoria and Albert Museum)

the meagre wages of miners, factory workers and farmhands
afforded little scope for luxuries. In the serried rows of terraced
and back-to-back houses and in rural cottages, the dry privy was
the norm. Some advocates simply oozed in recommendation,
one Charles Richardson specifying the following design in 1886:

### DRY PRIVY
Minimum Size
### FOR A COTTAGE

Built with 9in brick walls, and brick on edge flooring, 4ft 6in
by 3ft in the clear, as shown on the Drawing. It will take 4

cubic yards of brickwork, and may be built for about £5.

A Dry Privy may also be safely built as a lean-to against the back wall of the Cottage, by which means the cost of the front wall will be saved. The door will then be on the side. The back should, in all cases, join the garden bed.

It must always be borne in mind that the essential features of the Dry Privy are: firstly, that the droppings

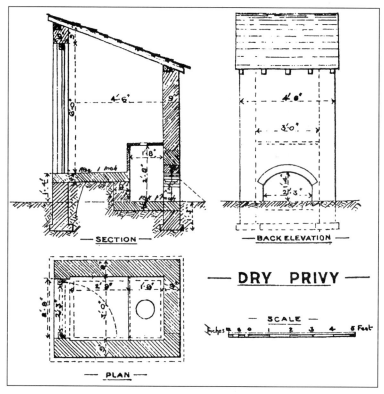

Charles Richardson's plan for his dry privy.

21

should be kept DRY, and secondly, that they should be kept ABOVE the surface soil.

For this purpose the floor of the Privy is raised two steps above the ground level, in order to form a 'catch' behind at ground level; the floor of this catch should slope slightly outwards, so that any moisture should naturally drain that way into a small heap of earth which has been tipped against the archway at the back.

The result of this arrangement is, that we are coming back to Nature, who has provided the surface soil to catch and purify all these things. We thus avoid entirely the formation of Sewage, and the consequent pollution of our wells, water-springs and rivers, and the propagation of fevers and zymotic diseases in general.

The Dry Privy requires no looking after, and is never offensive; all that it requires is that it should be emptied once every six months or so, and this is done without trouble in five minutes, when the earth and the droppings are shovelled out on the level and mixed with a little more earth, after which a barrow full of fresh earth is tipped against the archway, and that is all that is wanted. If what has been taken out is left in a heap for two or three weeks it becomes valuable manure for the garden.

Old-fashioned privies, instead of having the floor raised two steps above the surface, in order to form a 'catch' usually have cess-pits dug into the ground ; these are a mistake, for they hold water, and thus form Sewage, which makes a privy offensive and sometimes the cause of propagation of fevers around them; besides making the emptying

1898.]     SHEFFIELD ADVERTISEMENTS.     19

# GUEST AND CHRIMES,

## FOUNDRY & BRASS WORKS, ROTHERHAM,

### And 128, SOUTHWARK STREET, LONDON, S.E.

**PRIZE MEDALS.**

 **1851**

**52A.—WATER CLOSET AND FIRE COCK.**

| 1862. AWARDED. | 1862. AWARDED. |
|---|---|
| **Class 8.—FOR WATER METER, &c., SIEMENS'.** | **Class 31.—FOR WATER WORKS ARTICLES.** |
| "PRACTICAL SUCCESS OF WATER METERS, &c.; ORIGINALITY OF THE WHOLE." | "PROGRESS IN FABRICATION OF USEFUL ARTICLES FOR THE DISTRIBUTION OF WATER IN TOWNS." |

Agents at Hamburg:—Messrs. ALFRED BARBER and Co.
Agent at Brussels:—Mr. EDMOND LAMAL.

**BATEMAN & MOORE'S & CHRIMES' PATENT HYDRANTS OR FIRE COCKS.**
Single and Double Air Valves.
GUEST & CHRIMES' IMPROVED SLUICE COCKS, for Water, Steam, Sewage and Gas
(The body being cast in one piece).

**SIEMENS & ADAMSON'S PATENT WATER METER.**
Chrimes' Patent High Pressure Loose Valve Screw-down Cocks.
(Of the whole of the above G. & C. were the Original Manufacturers and Sole Licensees).
**RESERVOIR VALVES OF ALL DESCRIPTIONS.**
**REFLUX, RELIEF, AND PRESSURE REDUCING VALVES.**
CATHELS & TERRACE'S PATENT FOUR-WAY DISC GAS VALVES.
**CATHELS' PATENT DISTRICT DRY GAS GOVERNOR.**
**TERREY'S PATENT FEED REGULATING COCK.**
PATENT ABSOLUTE WATER WASTE PREVENTER.
ESKHOLME'S PATENT PNEUMATIC REGULATOR AND VALVE CLOSET.
Waste-Preventing Single and Double Valve Service Boxes.
**IMPROVED SELF-ACTING & PULL WATER CLOSET.**
**PEARSON'S PATENT LOCKING APPARATUS FOR BATH SUPPLY FITTINGS.**
LOWE'S PATENT EFFLUVIA TRAPS, BEGGS' IMPROVED. NEWTON'S PATENT STREET GULLY.
**F. SIEMENS' PATENT REGENERATIVE GAS BURNERS.**
**COWAN'S PATENT HIGH POWER GAS LAMPS.**
Patent Storm-Proof "ARC" Lamps for Gas.    "ARC" Lamps for Incandescent Gas Lighting.
**GAS CHANDELIERS, BRACKETS, AND FITTINGS.**
GOLDSMITH'S PATENT SIGHT WATER LINE INDICATING GAS METER.    ORDINARY WET AND DRY GAS METERS.
**STREET WATERING AND FIRE EXTINGUISHING APPARATUS**
Of every description, as HAND or DELIVERY PIPES, JETS, JET and SPREADER to distribute Water in imitation of RAIN;
HOSE COUPLINGS; LEATHER, INDIA RUBBER, GUTTA PERCHA, and CANVAS HOSE; COUPLING WRENCHES, &c.,
or any other Article made to order or size.
**PLUMBERS' AND GAS FITTERS' BRASSWORK OF EVERY DESCRIPTION.**
Drawings, Descriptions, Prices, and Testimonials will be forwarded per Post, on application as above.

ALL THE ABOVE ARTICLES MAY BE SEEN ON APPLICATION TO

## GUEST & CHRIMES, BRASS WORKS, ROTHERHAM;

Or to **THOMAS BEGGS & SON, 128, SOUTHWARK STREET, LONDON, S.E.**
Telegram Address:—"GUEST, ROTHERHAM."     (II)

The innovative Yorkshire firm of Guest and Chrimes patented a number of devices for use in water closet systems. Advertisement from 1898.

This 15th-century font is from a former Augustinian friary in Hull. At the Dissolution it was 'appropriated' to the local Tiger Inn where, suitably drilled, it served as a urinal. Miraculously, it survives today, residing in a garden in the village of Welton.

of them a very difficult and offensive operation. But the evils of these are as nothing with those of the water-closet.

## CHARLES RICHARDSON

There were dozens of variations on this basic design in Yorkshire, sited in communal yards and in gardens, the more refined devices being fitted with ash hoppers whose contents were discharged after each sitting. Some of these privies lived up to Richardson's high praise. Others, especially in the city slums, were straightforward breeding parlours for pestilence and disease.

Technology and main drainage eventually percolated as far as the rude abodes of the masses, 'automatic slop water closets' manufactured by the famous Burnley firm of Ducketts arrived on scene (more of these later) and by the early 1950s even I enjoyed the pleasures of an outside flushing loo...complete with a resident mouse.

And so to the multi-coloured, sanitised conveniences of the space age. What next? Computerised flushing? Self-cleaning bowls? Even-softer wipes? Such is the perfection of the modern WC, that I foresee only minor technological developments in the future, leading to the more efficient use of water and the introduction of new stay-clean materials. Apart from such refinements, there will be little call to incorporate anything else, apart, that is, for a whiff of nostalgia for the privies of old.

# [ 2 ]

## BY THE PRIVY DOOR

One of the most useful structures in the history of mankind, the privy was, nonetheless, the acme of austerity and functionality. Generally unadorned, save for a splashing of whitewash and a carefully applied scouring of 'donkey stone', it was likewise sparsely equipped, the only refinements, apart from an occasional battered chair, being a means of abstersion and a nail-bashed picture of royalty.

The cleansing medium for generations of Yorkshire folk was newspaper, although I am told that privileged types from the Holmfirth area who ingratiated themselves with local green-

Every self-respecting Yorkshire housewife donkey-stoned her privy step. Advertisement from *Waddington's Yorkshire Almanack* of 1924.

The editions featuring portraits of Hitler were particularly popular...

grocers employed fruit wrappings. Neatly torn into squares, usually by younger members of the family, the newspapers were threaded with twine and strategically hung within stretching

27

distance. Before the advent of the *Yorkshire Post*, the poorer Roman citizens resorted to stones and bunches of herbs and our own ancestors used sycamore leaves, mempiria (balls of rolled up hay), rags or, in coastal areas, conveniently shaped mussel shells.

For centuries paper was in short supply, but during the 18th century even classical authors were subject to the ultimate insult from privy users, the common practice of disembowelling books being celebrated in a popular poem entitled:

BUM-FODDER
for the
LADIES
a
POEM
(Upon Soft PAPER)
1753

The term 'bum-fodder' has since entered our lexicology as 'bumph'.

Commercial toilet paper eventually percolated into the British bog, the Drayton Paper Works of Wandsworth stealing a march on its rivals by producing palm size wipes 'ready stringed'. At first shoppers were too embarrassed to ask for the new product but blushes were spared by the use of plain wrappers. At the turn of the century, hard papers of the Bronco and Izal type cornered the market for some 30 years until the introduction of the hedonistic quilted tissues we know today. For some, the recent innovations have been a retrograde step. A number of correspondents recall highly educational visits to their privies, schooling up on history and world news by scanning pages, the haphazard assembly of which gave added spice to chronology and interpretation.

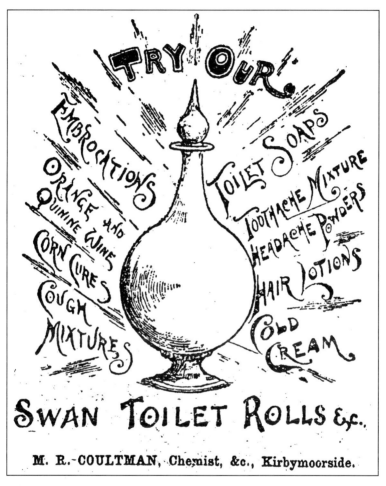

Advertisement in the Kirkby Moorside parish magazine for May 1920 (price 1d).

Dozens of envelopes hit the mat in regard to this sensitive subject. The following comments are typical:

I was very particular in what I used. Some papers were better than others and people had their own favourites. Mine was the *Daily Herald*. Magazines like *Picture Post* were usually left for kindling as they formed scratchy peaks and played havoc with your piles.

R. V. Martin
Driffield

I thought the *Sheffield Star* was the best. We had a two-holer – one for an adult and one for a child. There were two strings of paper. Children used a smaller size. I would often get absorbed in print and spend hours down there.

Roy Hartley
Barwick-in-Elmet

Although we had an inside lavatory upstairs, I much preferred to go outside. One pitch black night I dashed out without thinking, eventually realising I'd not checked for paper. I fumbled and felt something shiny and slippery which I took to be a magazine and wiped away. Next day, my son-in-law, who was a plumber, told me he had lost one of his putty wrappers.

N. Bell
South Elmsall

As a lad in Huddersfield I played a dangerous game. Mam would have killed me if she'd known. On cold mornings I'd drop paper down the hole and set fire to it. It was a real treat provided you watched the flames.

T. M. Morris
Scarborough

...nearby was a nail on which hung paper in neat squares. You could keep up with the previous week's news or radio programmes. Imagine the joy if it happened to be a selection from *Chips*, *Funny Wonder* or the *Comic Cuts* and the dismay if the concluding sheet of a particularly exciting piece had already been used up.

H. Wade
Chapeltown

I used to have a girl friend who lived in Filey around the mid 40s with a lavatory outside (earth closet). When possible I used to try and ask her mum if I could use it – reason – they had squares of *Dandy* or *Beano*.

B. Ashcroft
Filey

My uncle Amos was an engine driver for the LNER based at Dairy Coates in Hull. There were certainly no 'facilities' in the cabs in those days. On long hauls he did it on the fireman's shovel and said it burned wonderfully.

H. Covington
Market Weighton

# [ 3 ]

## PRIVY PONGS

It is an odorous fact, an inescapable reality – human waste stinks. And untreated concentrations, both liquid and solid, magnify the problem, giving off volatile, all-pervading vapours and attracting vermin and flies. Throughout the ages, stratagems and recipes have been devised to counter the gas but, surprisingly, revulsion has not been universal. In the old West Riding 'the stench was considered a most healthy perfume', a sentiment endorsed by the prominent Leeds surgeon C. T. Thackrah, who in 1821 reported that local night soil men found the nasal concomitants of their work quite enervating.

In the armoury of the pong preventer, positive siting and orientation were the most important weapons. Where possible, privies were located discreet distances from habitations, preferably downwind. This was easily achieved in rural areas where land was readily available, but in towns such as Sheffield, Leeds and Hull with their serried rows of back-to-back and terraced houses, isolating the nuisance was virtually impossible.

In the conurbations, little could be done about the proximity of pongs but small improvements in privy design helped vent the smells. Air grates were incorporated into privy walls and air holes, some in geometric or heart-shaped patterns, were cut into deliberately ill-fitting doors.

Cleanliness came next. Odours abhor old-fashioned elbow grease – that developer of the fearsome Yorkshire bicep – and cleaning continued until the operation drew blood. Poncing about with soap and water, however, never really caught on until recent times, so our erstwhile kings decreed that gongfer-

'There's a tremendous smell around here...' The author following up a nasal lead in Grassington. Photograph courtesy of Tom Markham

mors must work at night. And the shovelling continued in darkness right up to the present century, when the ritual of cleaning reached almost biblical heights. 'Cleanliness is next to godliness', trumpeted my grandmother, buffing up the woodwork until it shone. 'You could eat your dinner off my holes they were that clean', she boasted. And woe betide anyone who besmirched the seat, they soon experienced the power of grandma's biceps too!

In the repertoire of remedies, the final resort was chemical and biological warfare. The noxious whiffs were regularly dosed with carbolic, Jeyes Fluid or Izal, neither germs nor smells standing a chance against the onslaught of mop and bucket. Yorkshire housewives 'swilled', scoured and scrubbed their privies, whilst the night soil men used a defoliant tactic later employed by the B52 crews in Vietnam, 'squandering a

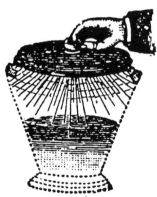
Nasty niffs neutralised for only six and a tanner ... post free.

huge pink cover of powdered disinfectant all over your yard'. Nature was also enlisted to the ranks, sweet-smelling shrubs and herbs such as honeysuckle, roses and lavender being encouraged to embrace the privy walls.

F. Biggin, of Askern, had the following to relate of how his mother dealt with the problem:

My mum was mustard with her carbolic and brush and we had few smells apart from the time a nephew came to stay. He had boils. Grandma was summoned and she mixed up her infamous 'Biggins Bombshell' – black treacle and something called flowers of sulphur. Little lad was petrified at the sight of that great dolloped spoon. It took some time to work through but Vesuvius had its way and the boils collapsed like barrage balloons. Grandad had been gassed in the Great War but said that the Yorkshire vapours were much worse.

The modern toilet is a mechanical device and like any other machine it is prone to cantankerousness and breakdown. Give me the reliable old privy any day. No problems with defective valves, leaking washers or renegade ballcocks there. Apart from the occasional splinter in the bottom and the odd rat or two – the latter were admirably exterminated by Samson, our Jack Russell – we had few complaints and no blinking water bills!

P. Simpson
Bedale

Finally, if all else failed, there were two last expedients – a pearl diver's breath or a peg.

There is an epilogue to this short chapter. Enterprising Japanese chemists have perfected a tablet to neutralise the odour of human waste. Marketed by the health food firm Dairin K K, the product has been snapped up by young kimono-clad Japanese women. Taken one with every meal, the confections erase the smell of faeces in just three days. The length of the Caucasian intestine suggests that two days will be the norm for Yorkshire persons, although at a good many pounds a box there are expected to be few takers. Not to be outdone by the orientals, a Yorkshireman has also taken up the challenge of cleaning up the gaseous act, Dr Colin Leakey of the Royal Hallamshire Hospital in Sheffield having developed a flatulence-free bean. His other brainwave is the 'flatometer', an instrument for measuring the after-blow of the more standard strain of vegetable. The contraption consists of a rectum applied washer connected by wine-maker's tubing to a balloon and an on-off tap. Up to 130cc of gas is the normal quantity of by-product collected over six hours, 'but a flatulent meal can', says Dr Leakey, 'give rise to an exceptional emission, which people at the Royal Hallamshire rather neatly call an episode. An episode can fill a balloon in just 20 minutes'. Patents are being hastily applied for before the Japanese miniaturise the device.

# [ 4 ]

## PRIVY EMPTYING

Waste from Yorkshire's country privies was held in the same esteem as farmyard manure. A valuable organic aid to soil fertility, it was spread wide and thick on farmland, allotments and gardens, producing bumper crops, one famous botanist proclaiming: '...land will take up this refuse and absorb it with impunity. Sewage can neither harm our soil nor its products. The roots of growing plants possess a power more subtle than the chemist's in disintegrating this matter and appropriating its most noxious ingredients to their own benefit.' In rural situations the availability and proximity of the tipping fields and the relatively small quantities of waste involved posed few problems, approximately 1 acre of land being needed to accommodate the excreta of 250 persons. In the population-swollen towns and cities, however, the burdens of disposal were acute.

It has been estimated that, in an average lifetime of 65 years, an individual produces over 4 tons of excrement and some 7,400 gallons of urine. In the crowded one-up, one-down terraces and back-to-back ghettos of the conurbations such quantities were deposited in one week alone, creating major health hazards and a disposal problem of truly oceanic proportions for the authorities.

In some urban areas, particularly along the river valleys of the West Riding, advantage was taken of nearby watercourses, gravity-transported excreta being delivered from the privies through flushless sewers. According to an 1852 General Board of Health Inquiry into public health in Wakefield, the privies 'are never flushed by artificial means; when necessary they are

The night-soil removers at this twin-holer at Kirkheaton had cleft feet – the business end was strategically placed over a pigsty!

Night-soil Nocturne ... local by-laws compelled the men to work in darkness. (BBC Hulton Picture Library from *The Complete Loo* by Roger Kilroy, Victor Gollancz, 1984)

opened and cleansed by manual labour. No use is made of the sewage; it is allowed to run to waste in the Calder.' So bad was the condition of this grossly polluted river, that in 1866 a complainant wrote in perfectly legible script to Sir Robert Rawlinson's River Commission, having filled his inkwell at Wakefield Bridge! Even as many years later as 1886, not a single West Yorkshire riverside town had attempted to resolve its sewage problems, the conditions becoming even worse in the drought year of 1887. 'The atmosphere along the Aire and the Calder', lamented one correspondent, 'became almost too foul for human endurance and the stygian currents reeked with gases.' In 1893 another observer described the condition of the Aire as 'a series of black fetid pools of sewage linked together from weir to weir, fed on the garbage of town sewers and trade refuse.' One year later came the West Riding of Yorkshire Rivers Act which made it an offence to discharge into any watercourse 'solid matter' and 'liquid sewage' (including 'unpurified urine excrementitious matter'). Denied the ready advantages of the river, many advocates rejected the novel but expensive solution of building treatment works in favour of practices adopted in the orient. 'The Chinese have indeed solved the problem', declared one Yorkshire editorial, rebutting the notion, 'but only by over-running their vast country with countless receptacles, stores and porters of ordure, so that, as travellers bear witness, one universal atmosphere of stink prevails.'

Spurred on by legislation, by increasing outbreaks of cholera and other decimating diseases and by a genuine drive to improve public health, sewage disposal and treatment infrastructures were eventually built. Until then a nocturnal army, the valiant night-soil militia, or 'wet dustmen' as they were known in the East Riding, held back the tide.

In the absence, in some places, of even the most rudimentary conduits of filth, waste was removed by hand, teams of men visiting, as they had done for hundreds of years, the middens and yards during the early hours as prescribed by local by-laws. They came equipped only with high-sided horsedrawn wagons, tongs, shovels and lanterns. Some men wore handkerchiefs, bandit-style.

The excrement tubs were removed from the privies with tongs and hauled up onto the vehicles. When full, the malodorous carts, spilling effluent all the way, were taken to the disposal points at the city limits, or, as was the case in York, the cargoes were off-loaded into barges for transportation downstream. The system in the lofty town of Richmond was to tip the effluent into the river Swale! In Hull tons of fertiliser were delivered to the market gardeners of Cottingham.

The unhygienic domestic conditions – some privies could only be emptied by carrying waste through living quarters – and the unregulated and random tipping inevitably compromised public health, and disease spread as a result of contaminated water and food supplies and explosions in insect and vermin populations. And it must be remembered that in the unenlightened Yorkshire of the Victorian period, the habit of emptying chamber pots into the streets was widespread. Many such thoroughfares were cleaned only once a year. A by-law to prevent this foul practice in Denby Dale and Cumberworth was introduced as recently as 1898!

Some idea of the colossal task of waste disposal can be imagined from examination of official records. The 1893 return for Wakefield gives the number of ashpits emptied as 9,173; the tally for 'excreta tubs' removed was 86,528. Faced with such everspated rivers of human waste, it can be readily understood why the demise of the privy – regarded with some affection and nostalgia in rural parts of the country – was greeted with almost universal relief in the cities, although the inhabitants of one of our large towns were a noticeable exception. Whatever were Hullites thinking of in the plebiscite of 1903? Why did ratepayers vote by 21,000 to 12,000 against the conversion to water closets? 'They should leave things well alone. I can't be doing with all these new fangled WCs. Besides, it'll cost us more brass.'

The little dunny was sent by a family of Yorkshire exiles living in Whitby, New Zealand.

# [ 5 ]

## PRIVY PRODUCTS

My father was a fervent admirer of the Sioux, who in exploiting
the buffalo even used its dung as fuel. Pa never resorted to eking
out our coal supplies but in all other things he was an ace conser-
vationist. By employing the back of his hand as a strop, he made
a shaving blade last six months. Conditioned by his incarcera-
tion in Stalag Luft 12, long after rationing he continued to dry
and reuse leaf tea. He sold our faded clothes to the rag merchant,
made leather pouches for our catapults out of worn down shoes
and used cut down stiffeners from old corsets as plant labels. But
it was in the garden that his organic instincts really came to the

A privy block in Barwick-in-Elmet. (Photograph courtesy of Rita Hartley)

fore. Onto that fecund plot he tipped ash and soot, and all our kitchen waste went on his compost heap, a sweetly humming mound supplemented by nail and hair trimmings and the contents of our privy, which, according to his dog-eared copy of *Beeton's Shilling Gardening*, puts heart into the land 'as bread and beef sustains and puts muscle into a man'.

Taking a 'shittuss scoop', he would ladle out the fertiliser onto a pile of cinders placed nearby. These would act as a filter and would, in a few weeks, 'sweeten' the mound ready for digging into carefully prepared trenches. Wasting nothing, he would also pour the contents of our potties onto his stack. He followed an established tradition, the use of urine in Yorkshire having a long history. World wide, its value in horticulture, in industrial processes, in medicine and in witchcraft has been attested for thousands of years. I would not wish to give our Inland Revenue any strange ideas, but in ancient Rome, Vespasian saw an opportunity of raising taxes by imposing a levy on urine, declaring that citizens in every street and alley must use receptacles strategically placed outside their homes. Those clever Sioux employed urine as a bladder alarm clock, consuming a specified amount of liquid before they slept, and across in Siberia the Chuckchee tribesmen would offer guests a cup of urine as a mouthwash.

Up to 1935 urine was used commercially in Yorkshire, a textile mill in Huddersfield so valuing the liquid that it was considered criminal for employees not to donate their own voidings. On a smaller scale, urine also figured in the manufacturings of a Halifax wheelwright in the 1940s and it is thought that some enterprising mill owners collected the commodity from local POW camps.

Urine was widely employed as a washing agent, when it was colloquially called wash or old wash. Lant was its alternative name on the Yorkshire coast. More colourfully, it was dubbed lee, chamber lee, scour, slops, old swill, wetting, netting, pee, piddle and piss, its endless applications making it a product too valuable to be poured away.

A strong alkali rich in nitrogen, particularly 'if it has been brewed overnight in the bodies of well fed citizens', urine readily removed grease from wool and was obviously important in both the domestic and the commercial production of cloth. In many a Yorkshire home the nauseating process of preparing newly woven pieces was carried on, the Reverend Easther describing how the cloth was laid out on cottage floor and 'lecked':

> 'A large kitful of urine and swine's dung was taken and strained through straw; it was then sprinkled on the cloth, and, as may be imagined, the smell in the house was horrible. As they lecked one piece it was laid down, and so layer on layer were placed in the form of a long parallelogram raised from the ground; then all the members of the household got up and trampled it! There it lay till morning; it was then wrapped up in a bundle, taken to Honley or the nearest place to a fulling mill; it was scoured, the offensive fluid washed out of it, and then it was brought dripping home...'

Urine was also a necessary ingredient in dye mixes, as can be seen from the facsimile of a 17th-century note left by the Fairfaxe family of Steeton and Denton – see page 46.

Indispensable to the successful operation of West Riding mills, urine had no chemical challengers until 1830 when the large scale production of ammonia was perfected in Huddersfield. Up to then it had reigned supreme. Any commodity in demand attracts a premium and urine was no exception. Some of my older correspondents remember being paid 1d per bucket for the stuff (redheads were thought to produce a superior pailful and got $\frac{1}{2}$d more). According to my measurements, the average

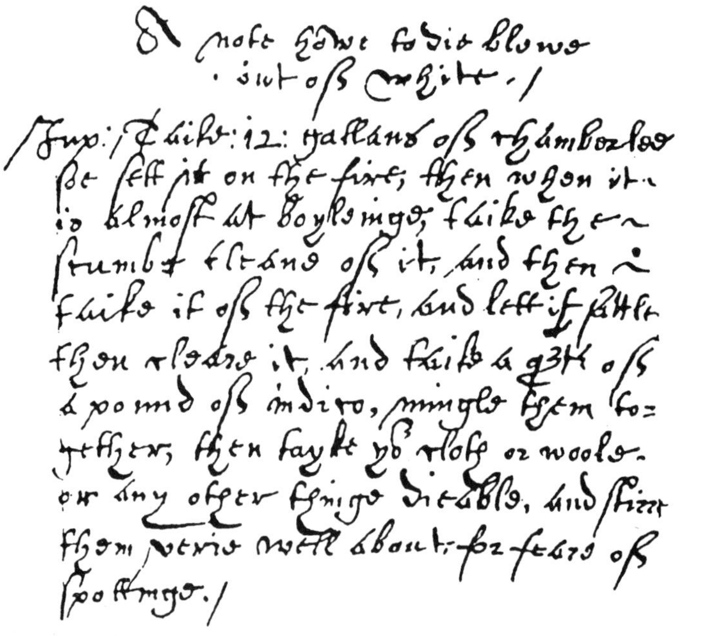

*[handwritten manuscript text reproduced in facsimile]*

A Note howe to die blewe out of white

Imp. Taike 12 gallons of chamber lee soe
sett it on the fire; then when it is almost
at boyleing, taike the scumb cleane off it
and then taike it off the fire, and lett it
sattle then cleare it, and taike a quarter of
a pound of indico, mingle them together,
then tayke your cloth or wool or any other
thinge dieable, and stirre them verie well
about, for feare of spottinge.

This 17th-century recipe uses 12 gallons of urine! (From the manuscripts of
the Fairfaxe family of Steeton and Denton)

adult voids $2\frac{1}{2}$ pints per day, so the combined tally for say six adults could amount to a sizeable 6d per week. The urine was collected inside homes in tubs, barrels, jars, buckets, cisterns or any other convenient containers or it was channelled into outside receptacles through spouted slop stones or lant outlets set into walls. There are notable examples of these lant stones in Langber, Linton-in-Craven, Coniston Cold, Adel, Wycoller, Riddlesden, Thornton, Silsden and Queensbury. Onward transportation was the responsibility of professional carters. For example, one 'Piss Dick' of Shelley went from door to door with a pony and wheeled barrel a 'weeting dob'. In Berry Brow, Huddersfield, the operation was carried out by 'Piss Joe' who wore a distinctive smock frock and a cap. Once collected, the urine was stored at the mills in large vats.

From the great mills, cloth went to all parts of the Empire. In Leeds the famous Benjamin Gott operated the Bean Ings Mill

Deserted and doorless. Redundant privies in Newsome Road, Huddersfield.

where dozens of gallons of urine were used every week, Gott recording details of the operation in his notebooks:

> The scouring pan is set in the following manner. Fill the Vessel with half urine and half water & as much sweet soap as will make it feel slippery & heat up to 140°. About this point you need not be very accurate – the cooler the water to make the wool clean the better. Put the wool in by six or eight pounds at a time & keep constantly stirring it for a few minutes till clean...as the Pan empties keep filling it up with ½ urine & half water. By this management the pan may be kept in order for a year & more. Indeed, it is better not to empty above three times in 2 years...

Other practical uses were legion, thousands of gallons going to the alum industry alone. Urine was essential in preparing the alum shales for use in tanning and dyeing. Brought in bulk from London aboard cargo ships and transported overland to large reservoirs near Whitby harbour, the urine supplied the extensive coastal works. The demand was insatiable. In just two months during 1612 the accounts of Sandsend operation show consumption at a staggering 28,288 gallons. As a lubricant, urine was essential in the wiredrawing industry and it had wide application in engineering. It was also used as a coolant and a caulking agent and as a means of hardening iron and steel. Its versatility did not end there, many Yorkshire folk believing in its therapeutic properties.

In Shipley around 1900 it was prescribed as a balm for bleary eyes. Bradfordian practitioners went one better, recommending urine as a cure for deafness and earache, whilst a herbalist in Honley near Huddersfield advocated a daily swig to energise the liver and spleen.

As a skin toner and cleanser, in the days before the general availability of soaps and shampoos, urine was often used. 'The second thing my grandma did when she got up was wash her face in t'po', boasted a Honley resident, proudly adding, 'she never had a wrinkle.' Such beauty treatment spanned the age gap, a Brighouse lady confiding, 'My mother would wipe a baby's face with a wet nappy to give it a lovely skin.'

In performing household chores, urine was without equal. Effective when mixed with bracken ashes as a pewter polish and in combination with hot water and a scouring stone for scrubbing floors, it also performed well as a stain and grease remover.

Finally, urine figured in the culture of youth. During the 1920s in Huddersfield, small boys played the exciting game of 'Fire, Fire' with newcomers. The raw recruit was told to throw down his cap and sprint to the next lamp post to summon the brigade. He was then instructed to rush back to assist the others, who had, meanwhile, valiantly hosed down the cap to prevent it burning to a crisp.

Sophisticated computer games and advances in chemical, detergent and pharmaceutical technology have today relegated urine to the status of an odorous waste product. But I am still reminded of the words of my father every time I flush away: 'There's gold in them there swills.'

# [ 6 ]

## PRIVY PREDICAMENTS

Privies have a predilection to awkward plights, that most colour-
ful of all expressions 'being caught with one's trousers down'
having its very origins behind the foot-wedged door. These por-
tals were cleverly hinged to open only inwards but, surprisingly
enough, this was one of the few stratagems aimed at repelling
boarders. Although latches were universally fitted, locks and
bolts were generally ignored, more subtle 'early warning'
devices being employed to maintain privacy. The noise of
crunched gravel alerted some lone sitters to proclaim their occu-
pancy by whistling martial tunes and visual signals also played a
part, deliberately undersized doors allowing would-be squatters
to kneel and peer, thus establishing the presence of tell-tale
undergarments.

'An accomplished tiptoer in my youth,' confides R. M. Boul-
ter of Harrogate, 'a boy who would rather eat sprouts than share
our two-holer with Aunt Ethel, I remember looking under the
door for those bloomers. Old "Parachute Knickers" always
wore khaki. She never ever heard me except when I giggled.
Then I'd run like hell!'

Many family members shared facilities, without any inhibi-
tions, the communal goings on two, three or even four-holers
generating welcome heat and bonhomie. Sharing with strangers
was, however, a less casual affair, as C. B. Richardson of Kirkby-
moorside recalls: 'As a young errand boy I was caught short at
Nafferton near Driffield. I asked to use the outside lavatory at
the railway station house. It turned out to be a 3 or 4 seater. I
had never used one before and to my horror, after a couple of

Interior of two-holer in Woodhead Road, Holmfirth.

minutes, the door opened and a little old lady came in. She said "Hello" and proceeded to use the toilet. I have never finished so quickly in my life and rushed out, flushing furiously. My father who was waiting in the butcher's van roared with laughter when I told him.'

What else went wrong in privies? Lots, according to the next crop of letters.

My aunt, who lived some distance away, came to visit our grandmother, but decided to go to the lavatory before coming into the house. Unfortunately, she opened the wrong door (two doors down) and found the gentleman of that house sat there. My aunt, never at a loss for words, said 'And how's your mother keeping?' I've told this tale many times over the years with much laughter.

O. Warriner
Middlesbrough

I was sat on the privy minding my own business when our neighbour – a big woman from all points of the compass – barged in and sat right on top of me! Being only a little girl, I was squashed down into the hole. It all happened so fast. There was no need to pull down our knickers in those days. Wearing 'two legs and a button' you only had to pop the button and spread your legs. Well, I got a right telling off and it was the first of many. The lady eventually became my mother-in-law.

C. Millington
Woodseats
Sheffield

We were given a new dog for Christmas. Always pinching stuff were Major – he was a bugger for robbing laundry baskets. Well, one day I was down the garden "mixing pudding" as we used to say and door blows open. In comes Major and makes off with my pants. It's a good job there was a scarecrow in the next field or I'd have been done for indecent exposure.'

K. T. Corntoft
Skipton

I'd just finished and reached out for the paper. All used up. What a pickle! I never knew it was possible with a McGowans toffee wrapper and three Leeds City Transport bus tickets.

H. Vause
Bridlington

I was a very young girl then. Excused from my lesson with the piano teacher I dashed for the outside toilet. To my amazement a tramp was sat there and he was so peaceful and sublime that I had not the heart to wake him. I tried to hang on but crossing my legs didn't work. Mum was so vexed.

S. Coultas
Pickering

The privy was our playroom. We played I Spy in there and it was perfect for Hide and Seek and Storming the Castle games. In later years, when paraffin lamps were replaced by torches, we engaged in another pastime – holding the light carefully between our knees and casting finger shadows of birds and animals on the whitewashed walls. Jim, the cocky one in the family, boasted he could create a beast beyond the talents of we mere girls, describing to us an elephant, trunk and all.

T. Hodern
Maltby

In the early 20s my parents had very little money so they shared a pair of dentures. Dad dropped them down the hole one day and had to rinse them off. Mother insisted on her own set after that. They're peculiar about such things are women.

T. B. Peacock
Pudsey

There is a final snippet from a gentleman who wishes to remain anonymous:

A big city gent came to the dales for a funeral. After the wake he asked to use the toilet and we sent him outside. A sniffy sort of bloke, he came back and complained about the smell. "And another thing", he said, "there's no lock on the door." This roused grandpa who'd been nodding by the fire. "We needs no lock yonder laddie", he replied, "I've lived here nigh on forty years and I've never had a bucket of shit pinched yet."

# [ 7 ]

## PRIVILEGED PRIVIES AND PISS POTS

The noble families of Yorkshire have always enjoyed an elevated status, their high stations symbolised by the use of purpose-built garderobes in an epoch when the plebeian classes squatted on the open ground. Splashings of the regal crud resulted in the miring of the means of ascent and all but the most determined scalers were deterred. Sitters were, however, vulnerable to attack, the pinked targets offering tantalising shots for archers.

For centuries our high roosters continued to fill the moats until the monastic influence caused some of the more progressive nobility to harness the cleansing power of water. Following the Dissolution, reredorters and conduits were incorporated into secular buildings, springs were diverted and tapped and rain-water run-off was used as a flushing agent linked to underfloor cesspits. Some privies incorporating the enlightenment of previous generations were built but legislation in the form of the Window Tax, imposed in 1696 and not repealed until 1851, ensured that these ill-lit and poorly ventilated smallest rooms had a poor reputation. And even these modest advances were the exception rather than the rule. Personal hygiene did not percolate the national consciousness until the 18th century and labour was, in any event, dirt cheap.

Gaily caparisoned close-stools – pierced wooden seats with removable excrement boxes underneath – came into widespread use. More discreet and less draughty than the privy shafts, they were emptied by servants who daily ran the gauntlet of polished stairways and irate masters who objected to their own smells. Spillage was a capital offence.

55

This elegant but utilitarian piece of bedroom furniture from the 1820s combines bed-steps and a close-stool with an integral creamware pan. (Courtesy of Temple Newsam House, Leeds)

Reacquaintanceships between dukes and droppings having become a loathsome reality, architects were petitioned to solve the problem. In the 17th century back stairways for the lower orders became commonplace, so that the gentry 'walking up the stairs no longer met last night's faeces coming down'.

The close-stool concept was gradually adapted and outwardly ordinary looking pieces of furniture – chairs, chests of drawers, bed-steps and even bookcases – were disguised to house the voidings, although polished mahogany and gilt handles never hid the smells from the brimful pots.

Pots. In Yorkshire, piss pots, potties, po's, jerries or goes under. Every household had one. A boon to mankind, especially in winter, the potty has, since its invention by the self indulgent Sybarites, been manufactured in every conceivable material. The Roman utensil was hewn from rare marble or fashioned from gold or silver. In England, earthenware, tin or pewter were used. By the early 19th century the design and decoration of pots became more elaborate, some famous pieces carrying portraits like those of Gladstone and Napoleon, whose visages could be desecrated in one carefully directed spray. One very popular pattern was marked with a large eye and a rhyme:

> Use me well, and keep me clean,
> And I'll not tell what I have seen.

Potties were kept close at hand in dining rooms and in salons and they were frequently used behind screens so that the convivial art of conversation could be carried on with decorum. But their use was not confined to domestic situations. Well organised travellers who objected to roadside mud and nettles had secret compartments built into their carriages. Underneath the seat

57

cushions of some vehicles were holes giving unimpeded access to relief. Peripatetic ladies took this comfort idea a stage further, using a glass device shaped like a gravy boat. Named after a preacher, Louis Bourdaloue, whose interminable sermons had females crossing their legs, bourdaloues were carried about in muffs, the device serving a dual purpose, being the original inspiration for the hand warmer. Presiding judges were also fond of their pots, finding them invaluable during long trials.

The chamber pot was an indispensable item of bedroom furniture right up to recent times but it had one over-powering drawback. Primarily the comfort of the starlit zone, it could hide brimful for hours, giving off emanations that reminded many a veteran of the Somme of trench warfare. The problems were so bad in the visitor trade that several local authorities had to resort to legislation. In 1932 the Borough of Harrogate enacted a by-law relating to boarding houses, compelling proprietors to 'remove all solid or liquid filth or refuse before the hour of ten in the forenoon of every day from every room in the house, and afterwards to thoroughly cleanse every vessel, utensil or other receptacle from such filth or refuse.' There was a further imperative. If the weather was not adverse, landladies had to keep 'windows fully open for two hours at least'!

Most po's have gone the way of the dodo. They were discarded, smashed up or sent for transmutation into munitions to lob at the Germans. A small number were kept under the bed for use by invalids and some still survive as plant or pot pourri pots, dogs' drinking bowls or museum pieces.

Few of my Yorkshire contacts have lamented the passing of what was once a universal household item. 'I was not sorry to see the back of my potty,' admits old salt T. Barraclough of Hull. 'Getting out of bed on frosty nights was a painful experience and although the pot helped ease the misery you never lingered too long. The porcelain was cold to the touch and after a

Cinders and slops — the routine of composting household waste still persists in some Yorkshire farmhouses.

while it was like sitting on a cheese wire. It left a deeply incised ring on your bottom and sometimes, when you'd had a few, docking was not quite Bristol fashion. And mops and buckets in the middle of the night are not conducive to a fella's love life.'

When I was seven years old, we moved to Cottingley Hall Farm, Churwell near Leeds. It was built in 1616 and it had a walled garden and a flagged back yard, then the farmyard. To get to the loo, we went through the yard and a back door into the garden and on up a path. It was a three-seater with a little one in the middle and each had a lid. Backing on to these in the farm-yard was another two-seater for the farm workers and on the wall in between was a little door through which were put all the ashes from the coal fires every day. It was called night-soil. They were cleaned out very often and the muck was taken away and mixed with the farm manure to be put on the land and ploughed in. The privy tops were scrubbed every week and disinfected.

L. Atkinson
Barwick-in-Elmet

# [ 8 ]

## PRIVY POETRY

The public lavatory, if I may stray into the communal arena of waste disposal, is the universal home of graffiti – that silent megaphone of the working man. As old as writing itself, this blowhole for pent-up angst or opportunistic vent for ribald humour is the supreme counter to hyperbole, waffle, newspeak and promotional bullshit. And it is free, spontaneous, anonymous, more humorous than *Punch* and more piercingly satirical than *Private Eye*, having an attentive readership of thousands.

Such is our perpetual need for occupation even when urinating that male relievers have, over the years, devised a one-

These jaunty public toilets on Victoria Pier in Hull have a nautical theme.

A valiant user of this cast iron Victorian urinal at Great Ayton ('thank goodness it's still open!') grimaces for the camera. (Photograph courtesy of Rita Hartley)

Magnificent urinals by Finch & Co of London underneath the King 'Billy' statue in Market Place, Hull. The glass-sided cisterns were once filled with goldfish!

Urinal stalls by J. Duckett & Sons of Burnley under Queen Victoria Square, Hull. The windows of the adjacent attendant's kiosk are hung with eulogies.

Space-age self-cleaning toilet in a Wakefield street. The sophisticated purifying system is supposed to operate only when the occupant has left.

handed routine permitting free licence with a scratcher or pen. The technique dates back to ancient times, notable examples of the scribbler's art turning up in the ruined cities of Pompeii and Herculaneum. The principal canvas for the craft has been the public lavatory wall, although ceilings, ceramic fittings, splash-backs, cisterns, toilet seats and even pipes and door handles have rarely remained unblemished. Abhoring the daub-free surface, assailants have, in response to powerful psychological upgush-ings, felt compelled to write and to doodle but, strangely, nobody has ever seen a besmircher in action.

The lavatorial academy of literature reached its zenith this century when municipal and railway station toilets were opened by the hundreds, one omnipresent slogan becoming sym-bolic of graffiti the world over. The phrase **KILROY WAS HERE** came from America, where James J. Kilroy was employed in a Massachusetts shipyard during the Second World War. An inspector of warships in a naval shipyard, he gave his personal seal of seaworthiness by scribbling the immor-tal words in chalk on every vessel. The practice soon caught on. Since the war, thousands of such classical one-liners have had their origins on lavatory walls but in recent years there has been a threat to such expressiveness. The recession and public funding cutbacks have led to the wholesale closure of our public conveniences, and in those facilities that have survived new resis-tant surfaces have been applied and advanced solvents intro-duced to cleanse away all traces of graffiti. Shame, that.

Privies and their products have, though, inspired more lyrical
tributes. Here is a selection, the first taken from a country newspaper around 1930:

> It is my firm belief
> That feeding through the leaf
> Will make all crops as healthy as can be;
> And after careful test,
> I find urine is the best;
> It feeds the plants and keeps them insect free.
>
> All plants do truly need
> A much-diluted feed;
> And this is how dilution should be done —
> To eight pints of water
> Add urine one quarter;
> In other words, just thirty-two to one.
>
> Sprayed gently on the leaf,
> Above and underneath
> It kills the pests and checks the mildew, too.
> The growth it seems to charm,
> And the flowers take no harm
> Sprayed once each week with one in thirty-two.

This next poem was originally read in East Riding dialect to a
live audience in Barmston Village Hall. It came to me via a
gamekeeper on the Wykeham Estate near Scarborough. Alas,
despite enquiries in Barmston, I have been unable to obtain the
poet's name.

## ANOTHER JOB

I'd gotten down to five feet deep,
To me it did look big;
But still me Dad weren't satisfied,
'Thee'll have some more to dig!

'It isn't as deep as old 'un,
That's almost full t'top;
When first we started using it,
You couldn't hear owt drop!'

I daren't dig outside them pegs,
Else new 'un wouldn't fit;
I couldn't see it mattered,
As long as you could sit!

But it seems that folks were fussy,
When it comes to Nature's calls;
I learnt you never had to dig,
Holes with slopping walls!

And ours went down to fourteen feet,
Afore me Dad said 'STOP!
I reckon that should do us,
It's a long way down from t'top.'

And what a do, when t'privy come,
All ready made to suit.
It was grandest yan in t'village,
That's why all folks turned out.

It had a special door on,
That would only open in;
And you had a pick of where you sat,
Because it was a twin.

A wood hook t'left o' door,
Was specially made to fit;
That's where me Mam would hang her coat,
And me Dad his belt on it.

You couldn't do that in t'old 'un,
Because there weren't a hook on t'door;
So whatever you took off in there,
It ended up on t'floor.

And another thing with that yan,
You hadn't to lark about;
'Cause if that door blew open,
It used to open out!

And it faced kitchen winder,
And folks in t'house would say;
'When we get that new privy,
We shall have to turn it t'other way.'

Why now we've got that privy,
Brand new and joiner made;
So we stopped using old 'un,
And used yan instead.

For first few days, all folks in t'house,
In turn would disappear;

Just to sit in t'privy,
All faking diarrhoea.

Now I remember,
How I used to sit with a grin;
With feet jammed against door,
So t'others couldn't gerrin!

To be first there in t'morning,
Often I would run;
And sit there making patterns,
In rays from t'morning sun.

I'd often wondered why they'd cut,
Two slots in t'top o'door;
Now I'd find out why they had,
The sun would reappear.

'How long's tha going to be in there?'
A voice down path would come;
'Only half a minute Ma,
I'm just wiping me bum!'

Now I know we had relations,
Aunts and uncles by t'score;
But some started to visit,
That I'd never seen afore.

Me Mam would go with ashes,
After t'fire had been lit;
And drop 'em down t'ole,
Where I alus used t'sit.

I can't see why she had to fill it up,
With bits of coal;
I think I'll get me shovel out,
And start another hole!

Finally, a little poetic tribute of my own:

### PERPETUAL MOTIONS

We got togged up for t'job in those days,
We dropped our kecks and bore the cold,
We sat aside and squeezed in tandem,
We spoke of tales, the like would freeze yer soul.

Dad talked of war, of wounds and khazis,
Of battles fought and comrades laid to rest,
Of secret muck as swelled his giant marrows,
'We're sat upon a goldmine, golden best.'

Business done, we'd reach for t'tearings,
Of *Yorkshire Post* and sporting green,
And then in t'pot, black ashes smothered
Best fertiliser soil has ever seen.

On Monday morns I'd take me spade and nosepeg,
I'd spread the clarty load on pea and bean,
On swedes and sprouts — down with yer clouts!
The rhubarb's kept us all in fettle clean.

# [ 9 ]

## PRIVY PROSE

In compiling this book, I became famous — especially with the postman — in the area of Barwick-in-Elmet, even an envelope marked 'BOGMAN' arriving unerringly, enclosing the following, from T. Groom of Easingwold:

I have one vivid and shining recollection of our privy. The purpose left gaps above and below its door provided ventilation. They were also perfect for lobbing earthworms, dead beetles, and on occasions live mice onto the laps of my dear sisters. They never needed laxatives.

Other communicants enjoyed sharing similar memories. I received two particularly illuminating letters from octogenarian Harry Wade of Chapeltown, Sheffield:

Our establishment was scrupulously clean with its well scrubbed floor and its white lime-washed walls. On entry, you were confronted by a pristine board on a five or so coarse brick support. It extended the length of one wall, offering the pantheon of its amenities, the choice of position being:

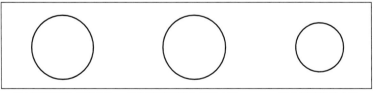

FATHER BEAR   MOTHER BEAR   or   BABY BEAR

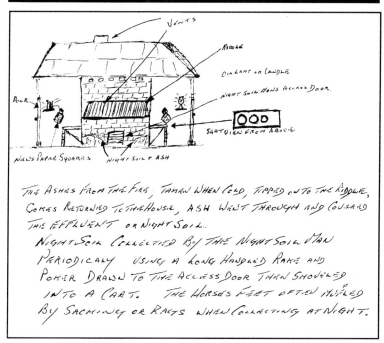

The annotated sketch reads:

VENTS

RIDDLE

OIL LAMP or CANDLE

NIGHT SOIL MANS ACCESS DOOR.

DOOR

SEAT VIEW FROM ABOVE

NEWS PAPER SQUARES     NIGHT SOIL + ASH

THE ASHES FROM THE FIRE, TAKEN WHEN COLD, TIPPED ON TO THE RIDDLE, COKES RETURNED TO THE HOUSE, ASH WENT THROUGH AND COVERED THE EFFLUENT OR NIGHT SOIL.
NIGHT SOIL COLLECTED BY THE NIGHT SOIL MAN PERIODICALY USING A LONG HANDLED RAKE AND POKER DRAWN TO THE ACCESS DOOR THEN SHOVELED INTO A CART. THE HORSES FEET OFTEN MUFFLED BY SACKING OR RAGS WHEN COLLECTING AT NIGHT.

'Our privy' — annotated sketch by H. Wade of Chapeltown.

plus a place to rest yourself if attending junior, or to place your washing or shopping basket ...

A great deal of pride and prestige was involved with the privy as it was usually shared with the people next door or more. Many a lad's girlfriend was checked on via the gossip grapevine. Did she clean well into the corners of the privy? Did her mother buy or bake bread? Failure on either account could spell doom to any romance ...

A strong bolt on the door was essential. If this vital part was missing, it was the usual practice of the incumbent to whistle or

Single-seater privy at Silsden. Notice the scythe ... and the face at the window?

sing loudly throughout the performance. Being a cherubic child of the times, I, along with others, carried a bottle cork in my pocket. When we noticed someone heading for the privy, we could race in front unseen and quickly pop the cork into the bolt keep. We could then hide nearby, usually bent double with laughter, enjoying the spontaneous fun. When the coast was clear, we would then draw lots to determine which one of us would retrieve the cork. The renditions of 'O Sole Mio' and 'Onward Christian Soldiers' were hilarious to a seven year old. The hymn singing in the privies was a lot less restrained than in the chapel on Sundays.

We as children used the privies as dens when playing 'Relievio' and 'Kick Art Can', but punishment would be dire if we were caught ...

When ma and pa wanted half an hour's privacy, usually Sunday after a good dinner, grandma would be steered and manoeuvred into the privy, then safely left for a while, apparently quite happy with her knitting. Grandma's repertoire consisted of marching songs from the First World War ...

One very dark night Joan just had to go, but she had no light. She picked her way gingerly down the path towards the privy, lifted the sneck and went inside. She shot the bolt, then seated herself quite comfortably all serene. Suddenly she felt something crawl up her back. She froze, unable to utter a sound. Further and further up her back the unknown horror climbed and it came to rest on her shoulder. A claw dug into her shoulder and she screamed, trying to brush it off. She recoiled and felt its scales and raced down the path horrified. As she reached the relative safety of the patch of gaslight, there was a rustle of feathers and a flutter of wings and the claws released their grip. Joan almost fell to her knees with relief as she recognised one of the next door neighbours' hens that had got out of its pen ...

I have been very remiss (*second letter*), having failed to advise you of the need for caution when entering the privy. To be sure that you didn't enter the premises a mere mortal and emerge a ghost, you had to first slake the ash in the midden with a bucket of water; the ghost being yourself wearing a coating of fine ash.

A cavalcade of such missives poured through my letter box for months, the postman, like a knowing wife who elicits infidelity through sniffs of her spouse's mail, always guessing the contents.

I would like to tell you of an amusing incident that happened to me during the Second World War. I was desperate for the loo, which was at the top of our garden on Scarborough Road, Fox-holes. As I sat, incendiary bombs were dropped behind Foxholes Manor and a piece of shrapnel landed nearly in my lap. I bent down to pick it up and promptly got my fingers burnt.

J. Windrass
Foxholes

I was a child in Scarborough during the war. We were on a day's outing when the sirens went. 'Quick!' my mother said 'let's take cover'. We did, running into the underground toilets at the top of Westborough (no longer there). Everyone was crowded in like sardines waiting for the all clear. Dark green tiles on the walls I remember.

B. Ashcroft
Filey

Privies all in a row in the cobbled backstreets of Grassington.

It was highly appropriate that I had a picture of the Führer in our privy-shed, it being eminently the best place for pulling faces. With a nail through his head he awaited an Allied victory. I remember that Stalingrad afforded me the most satisfying wipe I ever had.

J. Z. Smithson
Bradford

Back in the 70s my in-laws had a caravan in the select part of a well-known seaside camp. Imagine a long wooden hut, small windows very high up, just below the roof. The 'Ladies' were full length on one side, the 'Men's' on the other. There were three wash basins, minus plugs and a large white pot sink with meters to feed with 'bobs' before hot water spluttered out. Otherwise the basins had only a cold supply. The 'lavs' were over 20 years old, the wood well rotted in parts, with sunshine streaming through the laths. The inside was held together with cobwebs, hair, grass, birds' nests and sundry rubbish.

The walls of the 'smallest rooms' had a proliferation of wooden knots but many had been deliberately knocked out from the men's side. They did the same with the bunged up tissues which afforded us some privacy. Only one or two of the cubicles would stay shut and actually lock. The bowl itself was a few feet from the door so it was difficult to hover and lean forward with one leg outstretched to repel boarders. I hated having to use the hut especially during the night but with six of us sleeping in the van anything was preferable to the 'bucket'. A week at the coast was soul destroying for me. However, I discovered I was not the only one with these problems. Several relatives confessed to the same feeling as me — bloated.

P. Guest
Royston

Ours was just a one-holer. It was at the bottom of the 'yard', about 18 feet from the back door. When it was dark, we took a torch and both us children went. One would just sit and make up a story. To us children, the 'yard' was a long way off. I don't remember there being any real smell. It was mostly used by the women and children. The men went out in the fields whilst working.

E. I. Hawley
Withernsea

Sixteen houses in our yard, all just one up and one down, sharing two blocks of brick built outside toilets. Each block had four places with a great big steel grate where the daily ashes had to be emptied to cover the deposits of youngsters and parents (stools or pancakes?) The toilets were emptied during the night by lamplight into horsedrawn carts and taken to a dump in a quarry or on derelict common land. You knew to keep away from the stench from the huge pink cover of powdered disinfectant which was always squandered over your yard after a visit.

T. Shaw
Barnsley

We were on our honeymoon in Bridlington. She'd never seen a man before, so things were a bit awkward. Anyhow, we got back to the digs after a night out and she was desperate to go, but, you might know, flaming thing was engaged. 'You'll have to use the potty in our bedroom,' I explained, but she was none too keen on this. Eventually, after much pacing and crossing legs, she shouted, 'Turn round Tom and mind you don't look! And mind you don't listen neither!

T. Hewick
Ripon

'Room with a view' – two-holer at Addingham.

I was never really what you'd call a Mario Lanza but I often used to enjoy a good blow-out in our privy. The Royal Albert Hall was not a patch on that for echo. My version of *The Drinking Song* sent the allotment pigs bananas.

Q. Watkiss
Pocklington

I am now going back to 1927, and the following happened to me at the age of 5. What I am going to tell you took place at Skinningrove. It was an ironstone mining village and the street we lived in was called Albion Place and the houses were all company owned. Every house had earth toilets; ours had a wooden step about 9″ high to step onto and about 3 feet to where you sat with a hole about a foot in diameter cut out. There were no pans at the bottom but in the back street was a six foot door. Once a week at midnight two men with a horse and cart came, opened the door and shovelled the contents into the cart. Now to cut a long story short I lived with my grandfather, grandmother, two uncles Dick and Jim and aunt Beaty and mother and father. They heard a voice shouting 'Mam! Mam!' 'My mother says, 'That's our Arth' shouting', and when they did find me only my head was visible in the hole. You can just imagine what I was like! The times I had to listen to that story is nobody's business.

W. A. Womack
Saltburn

When I was at school in Hemsworth, the loos were dark and smelly and the walls were crumbling. They had pull cisterns and if I went in there when other people were in the building, I stood a strong chance of someone in the next cubicle standing on their loo and flushing mine from above — instant bidets!

P. Guest
Darton

81

High office has its little privileges — this single-seater was once reserved for a
Sheffield factory manager. The privy, complete with its original rather indis-
creet window, is preserved in the Abbeydale Park Industrial Museum.
(Photograph courtesy of Rita Hartley)

82

At Tankersley village school in the 1920s we had a communal toilet separated for boys and girls. There were six or eight cubicles with wooden seats over a common trough full of flowing water. At dinner time it got quite busy so you can imagine the to-do when one mischievous urchin set fire to a paper boat and floated it downstream. There were lots of shrieks and a hurried pulling up of knickers. We used newspaper in those days, ruffled up between your hands to soften it.

H. Gough
Tankersley

Grandma Rachel Bell was a cantankerous old flamer, forever fratching and shooing away the kids with a besom. But there was a poetic day of reckoning. One courageous lad got his own back by prodding a brush up the privy back passage as she sat sitting. His father was a chimney sweep.

D. Harwood
South Cave

All the nippers in our village sang this cheeky song ...

My father is a muckman,
He clears out the middens by night,
And when he comes home in the morning,
He's covered all over in sweet violets!
Sweet violets, sweet violets,
Sweeter than all the roses,
Covered all over from head to toe in sweet violets.

M. Garnett
Swinton

# [ 10 ]

## POISON PRIVIES

Faecal matter is a pudding of undigested pips, seeds, skins and highly fermented, bacteria rich, waste food. Without proper treatment and disposal, it hosts deadly germs, attracts insect and vermin infestation and releases toxins which, down the centuries, have killed people by the million. Massed populations led to mass deaths, even the Armada heroes succumbing to the 'bloody flux'. Battle casualties in 1588 were few, but almost two-thirds of our English sailors died of dysentery before ever returning to port.

In 19th-century Yorkshire the incidence of cholera and 'zymotic diseases' — smallpox, scarlet fever, diphtheria, typhus, enteric fever, measles and whooping cough — had a direct correlation to poor sanitation, and epidemics, especially within the poor back-to-back communities of the inner cities, were frequent. Other seemingly less virulent diseases claimed many more lives. It is sobering to record that diarrhoea, particularly amongst children, was often fatal.

In the 1840s, a single privy in central Sheffield could serve up to 20 families. 'The yards are unpaved,' reported one disgusted inspector, 'so that surfaces are little more than hard-trampled masses of excrement.' Little wonder then that the infant mortality rate was appalling. Even by the turn of the century the survival rate in some of the worst city ghettos was no better than 1 in 5.

All over the county, in burgeoning towns and villages, seepages from poorly constructed privies and cesspits led to polluted water and disease. In the winter of 1849, we are told, 108

A trio of privies in Back Lane, Silsden around 1889.

people died of cholera in Selby, with 19 fatalities in the union workhouse alone. The cause of the epidemic was rightly attributed to the defective state of the town's drainage and sewerage. Upon enquiry, it was discovered that the main drain had not been cleansed for over 45 years! In that same year, cholera and

19th-century sketch showing the filthy condition of a court off West Street, Hull.

diarrhoea in Hull claimed 1,860 victims in just four weeks.

The problems were not confined to the large towns. Right up to 1840 deaths from typhus were recorded in the parish registers of Muker in the wilds of Swaledale. In 1874 the same disease claimed several lives in Pateley Bridge, where the local townsfolk

This 19th-century drawing shows the appalling state of Robinson's Square,
New George Street, Hull.

took water from open street-side watercourses fouled with run-off from pigsties and privies. Later still, in 1877, Richmond was threatened with cholera, an official reporting: '... the houses are surrounded by all sorts of filth, both liquid and solid, often lying for months together, undergoing foetid decomposition, sometimes lying bare on the surface, sometimes held in receptacles ... but left unemptied for six months, unless there was sufficient to fill a cartload.'

Conditions were no better in Helmsley, the vicar, Charles Gray, being prompted into print after the death from typhoid of a favourite chorister: 'The only drain for the whole of the High Street is the Borough Beck; from the workhouse and all the houses all the way down, the whole drainage runs into it. It is simply an open sewer, bad at all times, but if ever dry, such a stench comes from under the arches, that it is plain there is enough filth to poison anybody.'

The majority of privy poisonings were amongst the working classes but in 1871 dramatic news from London showed that blue blood confers no immunity from infection.

On the 30th October 1871 His Royal Highness, the Prince of Wales visited Scarborough on a shooting trip. He stayed as a guest of Lord Londesborough in Londesborough Lodge on the outskirts of the town. At the time, the *Guardian* and the *Yorkshire Post and Leeds Intelligencer* were bursting with descriptions of cavalcades, firework displays and glorious days at the butts, but for reasons, presumably of propriety, no mention was made of a malady that afflicted the entire household. Unbeknown to the occupants of Londesborough Lodge, a water closet had been contaminated by effluent from a cesspit underneath the building. Lord Londesborough and two guests, the Earl of Chesterfield and the future King Edward VIII (together with a groom) ingested infected water and were struck down. The Yorkshire host soon recovered, but the Earl and the groom both died. Unwell, the Prince returned to Sandringham on the 4th November. For several weeks he endured a fever of a 'low and lingering' type until the 8th December, when the unmistakable symptoms of typhoid were diagnosed. For several days his life was in imminent danger. In churches throughout the land prayers were said, the 'petitionary vehemence' bearing fruit on the 14th December when the invalid began to recover.

Today, flushing toilet systems, washing facilities and a greater awareness by the public of the need for hygiene and cleanliness have virtually eradicated the scourge of the disease associated with the old privies, but calamities continued to occur until comparatively recent times. In 1932, following the cracking of a pipe, foul water contaminated the Square Wood Reservoir and typhus-infected water entered every house in Denby Dale. And even today illness is just a missed hand scrub away.

# [ 11 ]

## Privy Progress

White-hot technology in Yorkshire brought us water-powered looms, the steam engine and blast furnaces and with the mechanical revolution came advances in privy design, relegating the 'hole-in-the-ground-with-a-shed-on-top' concept to history. But the luxury of heated toilet seats had to tarry awhile, for in these northern nether regions evolution proceeds but slowly. First they gave us a bucket.

In some northern towns iron or tarred oak pails were strategically placed under the closet seat. When nearly full at the end of the week, the buckets would receive a dusting of dry matter. The ashes of anthracite coal were particularly recommended for this purpose, 'but the ashes of bituminous coal must be sifted and wood ash must not be used.' Finally, the mixture was consigned to a ditch or pit. Buckets were replaced in Mark 2 versions of this arrangement by slide-out drawers, and hoppers were fitted above the receptacle, automatically delivering a measured layer of ash when the privy seat was raised.

Flushing water closets gradually ousted dry privy systems, although in places progress was painfully slow. Even in the avant-garde environs of 1912 Harrogate, 50 privies and earth closets were in daily use. And the undoubted improvements were not universally welcomed, some aficionados of the arid zones still proclaiming their superiority to this day. One of the most fascinating tributes to the old privies comes from the famous Rowntree family of York:

My great grandfather William Rowntree (1806–1901), built a

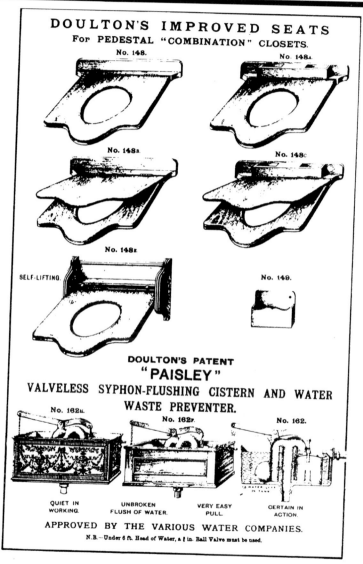

Are you sitting comfortably? Extract from Doulton's catalogue of 1898.

house in Scarborough in 1852. The house, known as Westwood House, was furnished with fashionable mid-Victoriana following the Great Exhibition of 1851 and was said to be the first house in the town to possess an indoor flush lavatory. Great grandfather Edward Stickney (1773–1863) refused to use the indoor toilet as he found it quite indecent.

P. Robson
Scarborough

Water closets quickly appeared in the larger, more affluent households but they were not generally installed in modest Yorkshire homes until just before the Great War, the popular prejudice being 'they waste water and put up the rates'. Many of my Yorkshire correspondents remember the awesome day of installation, the feelings of claustrophobia and loneliness and the sudden realisation that here was a chamber whose acoustical properties were totally unsuitable for singing! 'It took a long time getting used to I can tell thee.'

A transitional form of device was the Duckett, built by a firm of the same name in Burnley in the early 1900s. An 'automatic slop water closet', the Duckett utilised waste water from kitchen sinks to flush WCs, the device incorporating a pivoting self-acting tipper, triggered to overbalance when a given quantity of water had been collected. Directed in piping, often over a considerable distance, the flood of water would carry away deposits in the privy pan — 'and they never froze up'. In 1913 Ducketts advertised several models in their range, selling at between £1.10s.0d and £2.0s.0d, giving reservoir capacities of 2, 3 and 4 gallons. Some memories of these devices rank alongside nightmares of wartime ironclads and zeppelins:

We had a house in Hartoft Street in York where the comedian Frankie Howerd once lived. We had what was then known as a 'ducket' lavatory. I know I was never allowed to use the thing without my mother being there because the thing was very deep — like a well.

Mrs I. M. Hill
York

Kids said our 'ducket' was bottomless and home to giant rats. We never lingered, preferring to read our comics on the recreation.

S. Myers
Goole

I was frightened rigid. It had so many moving parts. After the old fashioned privy it was noisy and quite sinister.

B. Levington
Ossett

Other evocations are more amusing:

One day, the man next door came dashing into our kitchen and shouted, 'Don't put any water down! I've just been sick and lost my teeth down the ducket; must get them out.' And he did!

Towards the 1950s, I suppose things were wearing out, and sometimes my father had to poke down the ducket an old prop to tip the mechanism over. After we watched the Queen's coronation on television, we dubbed my father 'Clerk of the Closet' after one of the officials at the ceremony. He didn't think this was very funny.

When my brother was about 9 or 10, he and his pals would stuff paper down the ducket and set fire to it. It really made a wonderful roaring noise.

You had to be on reasonably good terms with your neighbour, and one wife washed it out one week, and the other wife the next week. You just hoped to live next door to someone 'clean'.

B. Holling
Monk Bretton

The ducket system was flushed by means of water draining from the kitchen sinks of more than one property ... because of the loud rumbling noise of the flushing operation it brought about a rather pleasant pastime for a seven year old. We would lie in wait for my younger sister or one of her friends to head in the direction of the toilet. We would then rush into our respective houses and turn on the kitchen taps full bore waiting for the loud roar of the flush and the even louder screams of our victims as they rushed from the toilet. Then, laughing our heads off we would shout 'pink 'uns!' If our ruse succeeded we were rewarded by their looks of consternation along with a hurried straightening of dresses. If, however, we had been rumbled, the girls would glare at us and reply, 'wrong then see', sticking out their tongues to the full length.

H. Wade
Chapeltown

The technological 'halfway house' in the story of sanitation is, apart from a few scant references, almost lost to history. Examples of privies, many crumbling but some restored to glory, still exist but of the Ducket, in the course of my searches, I have found no trace. Pity that. 'Just Williams' everywhere have been deprived of so much fun.

Front Street, Castleford — a rare example of a cast iron urinal made by the Saracen Foundry in Glasgow by Macfarlanes — circa 1880. Inspired by the Parisian pissoir. A listed structure, it was proposed for demolition by the local council in 1994 but over 200 local residents petitioned for its preservation.

# A Privy by any Other Name

(The term derives from the Latin word 'privatus' meaning apart or secret.)

Biffy
Bog
Boghouse
Bombay
Chuggie
Closet
Comfort station
Craphole
Crapping kennel
Dike
Dinkum-dunnies
Dunnekin
Dunnick
Dyke
Garden loo
Garderobe
Gong
Gong house
Heads
Houses of parliament
Jakes
Jerry-come-tumble
Karzi
Klondike
Latrine
Lavatory
Little house
Nessy
Netty
Out the back
Place of easement
Reading room
Shit-hole
Shit house
Shittush
Shooting gallery
The chapel of ease
The grot
The gun room
The hum
The ivy house
The long drop
The necessary house
There she blows!
The slash house
The sociable
The thinking house
The throne room
The you know where
Three and more seaters
Thunder box
Widdlehouse